Either Right Or Human

Abhijit Naskar is a celebrated Neuroscientist, Bestselling Author of 100+ books, World's Beloved Poet of 1000+ sonnets, and an untiring advocate of mental health and global harmony, who has been serving at the forefront of humankind's struggle against hate, intolerance, bigotry and fanaticism.

Either Right or Human

300 Limericks of Inclusion

ABHIJIT
NASKAR

Either Right or Human: 300 Limericks of Inclusion

Copyright © 2023 Abhijit Naskar

This is a work of non-fiction

An Amazon Publishing Company, 1st Edition, 2023

Printed in the United States of America

ISBN: 9798865776673

Fabric of Humanity
Build Bridges not Walls: In the name of Americana
The Constitution of The United Peoples of Earth
Lives to Serve Before I Sleep
When Humans Unite: Making A World Without Borders
All For Acceptance
Monk Meets World
Mission Reality
Citizens of Peace: Beyond The Savagery of Sovereignty
Operation Justice: To Make A Society That Needs No Law
See No Gender
The Gospel of Technology
Every Generation Needs Caretakers: The Gospel of
Patriotism
Aşkanjali: The Sufi Sermon
Mad About Humans: World Maker's Almanac
Revolution Indomable
When Call The People: My World My Responsibility
No Foreigner Only Family
Hurricane Humans: Give me accountability, I'll give you
peace
Ain't Enough to Look Human
Servitude is Sanctitude
Time To End Democracy: The Meritocratic Manifesto
I Vicdansaadet Speaking: No Rest Till The World is Lifted
Boldly Comes Justice: Sentient not Silent
Good Scientist: When Science and Service Combine
Sleepless for Society
Neden Türk: The Gospel of Secularism
Martyr Meets World: To Solve The Hard Problem of
Inhumanity
The Shape of A Human: Our America Their America
When Veins Ignite: Either Integration or Degradation
Heart Force One: Need No Gun to Defend Society
Solo Standing on Guard: Life Before Law
Generation Corazon: Nationalism is Terrorism
Mucize Insan: When The World is Family
Hometown Human: To Live For Soil and Society
Girl Over God: The Novel
Gente Mente Adelante: Prejudice Conquered is World
Conquered
Earthquakin' Egalitarian: I Die Everyday So Your Children
Can Live
Giants in Jeans: 100 Sonnets of United Earth

Vatican Virus: The Forbidden Fiction (Abi Naskar
Adventures Book 2)
Karadeniz Chronicle: The Novel (Abi Naskar Adventures
Book 3)
Şehit Sevda Society: Even in Death I Shall Live
Handcrafted Humanity: 100 Sonnets For A Blunderful
World
Mücadele Muhabbet: Gospel of An Unarmed Soldier
Making Britain Civilized: How to Gain Readmission to The
Human Race
Dervish Advaitam: Gospel of Sacred Feminines and Holy
Fathers
Honor He Wrote: 100 Sonnets For Humans Not Vegetables
The Gentalist: There's No Social Work, Only Family Work
Either Reformist or Terrorist: If You Are Terror I Am Your
Grandfather
Woman Over World: The Novel (Abi Naskar Adventures
Book 4)
High Voltage Habib: Gospel of Undoctrination
Bulldozer on Duty
Find A Cause Outside Yourself: Sermon of Sustainability
Ingan Impossible: Handbook of Hatebusting
Amor Apocalypse: Canım Sana İhtiyacım
Amantes Assemble: 100 Sonnets of Servant Sultans
Mucize Misafir Merhaba: The Peace Testament
Divane Dynamite: Only truth in the cosmos is love
Sin Dios Sí Hay Divinidad: The Pastor Who Never Was
Corazon Calamidad: Obedient to None, Oppressive to None
Esperanza Impossible: 100 Sonnets of Ethics, Engineering &
Existence
Mukemmel Musalman: Kafir Biraz, Peygamber Biraz
Himalayan Sonneteer: 100 Sonnets of Unsubmission
Yarasistan: My Wounds, My Crown
The Centurion Sermon: Mental Por El Mundo
Her Insan Ailem: Everyone is Family, Everywhere is Home
Humankind, My Valentine: World's First Anthology of 1000
Sonnets
Aşk Mafia: Armor of The World
Vande Vasudhaivam: 100 Sonnets for Our Planetary Pueblo
Visvavictor: Kanima Akiyor Kainat
Sapionova: 200 Limericks for Students
Rowdy Scientist: Handbook of Humanitarian Science
Insan Himalayanoğlu: It's Time to Defect
Tum Dunya Tek Millet: Greatest Country on Earth is Earth

DEDICATION

For Humankind, and to any lifeform
in time and space
wanting to know humankind.

CONTENTS

Note to Future

If at some point in the future, the "right" successfully mends its bigoted tendencies, or even shows substantial initiative for it, you are to republish this work, with the subtitle "300 Limericks of Inclusion" as the title, replacing the current title "Either Right or Human".

Part 1

1.

Left or not, is irrelevant -
Either right or you are human!
Leaving the tribal days behind,
Wield your inclusive heartlight.
Ever onward with warmth and reason!

2.

Long and hard I tried to stay aloof,
From all dilemma and charade of cahoots.
Seeing most inhumanity lean to one side,
Justice and neutrality start to collide.
Real insight lets no backbone to stoop.

3.

More you understand science and sapience,
Harder it is to believe in a being omniscient.
More you realize the endemic inequalities
of society - all the prejudice and biases,
Harder it is to stay neutral and indifferent.

4.

Insight makes you restless,
Insight makes you sleepless.
While the indifferent sleep,
as but intellectual sheep,
Brave lions struggle ceaseless.

5.

Struggle, struggle, and struggle again,
Struggle till all bigotry is forgotten.
Intellect mustn't facilitate indifference,
Ignorance mustn't facilitate compliance.
Prioritize humanity over allegiance inane.

6.

Pledge no allegiance to ideology,
no allegiance to intellectuality.
Abandon intellect if needed,
abandon ideology if needed -
Never let nothing overcast humanity.

Part 2

7.

The greatest idea is humanity,
The greatest belief is humanity.
The greatest wisdom is service,
 greatest philosophy is service.
In service we realize humanity.

8.

Service is not left, but human.
Equity is not left, but human.
To be inclusive is to be human,
To defy intolerance is human.
Love is not left, but human.

9.
Justice is no exercise in ideology,
Justice is an exercise in humanity.
Acceptance is act of the human half,
Intolerance of the animal half.
Upon your choice hangs humanity.

10.
Animals end up as animal remains,
Humans live beyond bodily chains.
Flesh and bones may wither,
Character with ideas don't disappear.
Life isn't lived till lived beyond chains.

11.

My immortality needs no make-believe,
To such superstition never you pay heed.
Fools chase after reincarnation,
The wise but embody ascension.
Time after time the mission is relived.

12.

I am life, I am light -
What is death to cause me fright!
I eat death for breakfast,
suffering for supper.
Death affects body, not mindlight.

Part 3

Gods Don't Pray
(The Sonnet - 1253)

13.
Bible without benevolence is bogus,
Church without reason makes SCOTUS.
Faith without common sense,
and intellect without sentiment,
are both equally dangerous.

14.
Knowledge begins where rigidity ends,
Justice begins where indifference ends.
No nonviolence ever reforms a tyrant,
You must stand up bold and fervent.
Without the blood of Bose and Singh,
no Gandhi could've claimed independence.

15.
You can wish and pray all you want,
It doesn't change the state of the world.
World reforms when you take charge,
stepping out of your castle of glass,
as the janitor sleeps world becomes junkyard.

Wishes and prayers are the coward's excuse
for brainless incompetence and spineless impotence.
Awake, Erupt, O Vanguard Volcano!
Gods don't pray - Gods are the answer sapient.

16.
Gods don't pray in wishful indifference,
Gods are the answer ultimate and sapient.
Awake, Erupt, O Volcano Vanguard -
Take no cue from ancient scriptures.
Person's gospel is but their own conscience.

17.
They say scripture is infallible,
That's more reason it is expendable.
Better shelf a scripture,
than ruin a dreamer.
Bell tolls for the rules of dead people.

18.

Any book can suggest anything,
All is suggestion, nothing doctrine.
Take what works today,
The rest you must throw away.
Never take no one as authority supreme.

19.

Don't confuse expertise with popularity,
Don't confuse tradition with humanity.
What's tradition might be inhuman,
What's popular might be a violation.
To be human is to discard animal loyalty.

20.

When ancestors peddle prejudice,
They are but begging to be buried.
Let them live their life,
as they believe and wanna die,
But let no life be driven by antique.

Part 4

21.

New world needs new drivers,
New world needs new thinkers.
Putting aside all old thinking,
all charm of bigotry most blinding,
Reject the hate and resume the healing.

22.

Old is not necessarily inhuman,
But old is no measure of what's human.
Life must decide its own parameters,
History provides lessons, not measures.
Not old or new - human must live as human.

23.
To look human is no brainer,
To behave human is another matter.
With makeup even a chimp looks human,
yet it lacks human warmth and reason.
Don't be a good-looking chimp, be better.

24.
Enough learning, enough investigation,
When will you embark in expansion!
Pioneer is the path,
Pilgrim is the pilgrimage.
World unity stems from expansion.

25.

I don't write on integration of cultures,
I am the integration of cultures.
The pioneer is the path,
The poet is the poetry.
When will you stand as bridge
between worlds?

26.

Expansion brings unification,
Contraction brings castration.
Bigger the mind, smaller the world,
Rigidity causes disease and dirt.
Mind and world are one living organism.

Part 5

27.
The living must evolve,
While the dead make mob.
Pause in evolution
is cause of extinction.
Without motion, life it is not.

28.
To grow you must live,
To live you must grow.
Think with some heart,
Feel with some head.
To live is to grow.

29.
Brainy heart or hearty brain,
Find unison between heart and brain.
Brainless heart and
heartless brain,
are equally useless and inane.

30.
Inequalities are result of rigidity,
often justified as traditional sanity.
Such sanity is root of insanity,
in other words, it's inhumanity.
Sanity starts with awareness of insanity.

31.
I am a behaviorist,
My own worst critic.
I question myself more
than my haters rave and roar,
Facing million questions
mind morphs cataclysmic.

32.
We cannot aim for the stars,
with our mind smashing rocks together.
Abandon the rocks,
abandon the caves -
nuts and bolts achieve nothing
if heart's crippled by fear.

Part 6

33.
It's okay to live with fear,
what's not okay is to live in fear.
Let the fear be as it is,
Pay neither submission nor heed,
Step out of the cave, morning will appear!

34.
Night and day are made of mind,
Light and dark are born inside.
Worse than ignorance
is illusion of knowledge,
which keeps apes from being civilized.

35.
Civilized are those who are ever aware
of the ignorance they eternally bear.
Self correction distinguishes
human from the animals.
Correct your past, your future will appear.

36.
Correct prejudice to patience,
Correct biases to benevolence.
Correct war to peace,
Give yourself a new lease.
Correct savagery to sapience.

37.
War is the status quo,
Peace is a political woe.
Up the creek without a paddle,
Better not rock those in the saddle,
Lest you are branded a stately foe!

38.
If you still got the backbone,
To tell right from the wrong.
Grab the keys from savages,
Trash all prehistoric baggages!
Past tradition, stand just and strong.

Part 7

39.
Nations are not handed perfect,
They are perfected by hand.
Society is no factory product,
Society is but handicraft.
Craft with care as your flesh and blood.

40.
To care for the world isn't political,
To care is to be human - plain 'n simple!
If you did not care,
that's the real disaster.
Responsibleness makes all cruelty crumble.

41.

I prefer responsibleness over responsibility,
The former indicates action, the latter theory.
Till indifference is a thing of the past,
all talk of law and order is futile fuss.
Till accountability is first nature,
all order is imaginary.

42.

Stand on your feet in matters of justice,
without all the law-abiding paralysis.
If you can't tell right from wrong,
without the help of constitution,
you won't be free from the reign of prejudice.

43.

If you can't tell right from wrong,
without scripture or constitution,
the entire library of congress
for you is but worthless,
books can't teach chimps to be human.

44.

Monkeys play smart, lion plays dumb.
Vermin play alive, volcano plays dead.
Develop your backbone in silence,
Sharpen your faculties without noise.
Let out the beast only when needed!

Part 8

45.

Action is the greatest prayer,
Inaction is sheer disaster.
Sit and pray all you like,
that will not bring light.
Light begins at the end of prayer.

46.

Where prayer ends and practice begins,
Where illusion ends and action begins,
There, beyond all textual comfort,
outside the bubble of dutiless thought,
life unfolds as the living intervenes.

47.
Life unfolds when the living intervene,
Civilization unfolds as the civilized intervene.
There is no modern world
without responsible act and thought.
Paradigm of indifference is a paradigm of fiend.

48.
Reformation 101: I am responsible.
Advancement 101: First human, then reason.
Insight 101: I know best what I know not.
Integration 101: Exist, I do not.
Interfaith 101: My faith is to listen.

49.
If all you can think is,
how great your culture is,
your opinion is trash,
better have another bash.
Where the ape ends, human begins.

50.
If all you can think is,
how great your religion is,
your opinion is trash,
you're anything but religious.
Where organized religion ends
real religion begins.

Part 9

51.
If all you can think is,
how great your nation is,
your opinion is useless,
just a primitive vestige.
Where nationality ends humanity begins.

52.
For your opinion to have some value,
it doesn't need to be logically true,
but it must have some basic humanness,
with a touch of the common sense,
only then the ape is born a human anew.

To struggle for a world free from bigotry and prejudice, is an eternally tedious process. Even when you eliminate from society the bigotries of today, the struggle won't be over - for then your mind will suddenly be aware of further bigotry that never appeared to you as bigotry till that moment.

So, you must never lose heart. For example, after everything I have worked for over the years, people unfamiliar with my work still ask me, do I support the lgbt movement? And with my habitual patience, I respond - what's there to support! Do you support people drinking water? Water is not something you support or don't support - water is the fundamental of life. Likewise, love is not something you support or don't support - love is the bedrock of life - or better yet, love is life.

53.
Love is the rock of life,
Love is the root of life.
Some drink water from cup,
Some drink water in glass.
Both equally sustain life.

54.
Support or not doesn't matter,
There is no life without water.
Some truths are beyond opinion,
unchained by petty tradition.
Only fools define truth by scripture.

55.
Sure, scriptures do have a value,
Just as all human literatures do.
All doctrines are born of mind,
a mix of both cruel and kind.
No ritual deserves more respect
than human rights do.

56.
Rights before ritual, heart before habit.
Love before law, truth before twit.
Love alone can illuminate love.
Hate is the vulture, love is the dove.
Pay attention to human welfare
over and above the holy writ.

Part 10

57.

Baseball builds more character than bible,
Gardening makes more gentle than bible.
Replace bible with any scripture,
there is no difference whatsoever.
No text, no matter the nature, is infallible.

58.

Reasoning is needed, tolerance is needed.
More than all, whole awareness is needed.
Indoctrination repels awareness,
Awareness doesn't let you be indoctrinated.
Best subjects for indoctrination are the dead.

59.
Death and indoctrination are one and the same,
Life and awareness are one and the same.
Be aware in being alive,
across predispositions uncivilized.
Awareness and wholeness are one and the same.

60.
I don't wanna rule nobody,
I don't wanna indoctrinate nobody.
But if your doctrine ruins another's rights,
behind the excuse of imaginary sacred light,
I shall be your worst blasphemous enemy.

61.

Only cowards try to make no enemy,
While bravehearts end up with plenty.
To stand on conviction,
is an act of the human,
but for a caveman it's not compulsory.

62.

Stand on conviction right through apocalypse,
Bend not an inch to please the elitists.
Light will come, lift will come,
Piercing darkness dawn will come,
So long as to inhumanity you never submit.

Part 11

Heart is my gospel,
brain is my constitution.
Backbone is my law,
service is my salvation.

My ethnicity is empathy,
my race is reform,
My nationality is oneness,
my name is human.

Mi etnia es la empatía,
mi raza es la reforma,
Mi nacionalidad es unidad,
mi nombre es humano.

63.
My name is human, my life is human.
No other identity is higher than human.
Take pleasure in your sects if you may,
from those prehistoric days.
There is no tradition higher than human.

64.
Human you are, human you must behave,
everything else is just trivial noise.
Even an ape is well aware,
who is family, who is stranger.
It takes a human to take the world in embrace.

65.

To find the globe in oneself is not globalism,
To find society in oneself is not socialism.
It is just a human behaving human,
coming forward past chimply division,
not afraid to chance the snare of barbarism.

66.

Globalism means global organism,
Socialism means social organism.
Put all dead dictionaries aside,
into your thoughts pour some life.
New world needs new breath and reason.

67.
Breath of all is the breath of one.
What's there to call for argumentation!
It's enough to just be a human,
be a human and stay a human.
Reformers got no time for argumentation.

68.
Argue not, engage not -
Do your duty, without support.
Who comes, who does not,
it is of no significance.
You come forward, that's enough!

Part 12

69.

Enough with bigoted holy water!
Enough with intellectual ice water!
When will the heart carry blood,
to deliver warmth across the world!
When will you stand to clean the sewer!

70.

Books don't bear miracle, breaths do.
Hate don't depict holiness, hearts do.
You are all the messiah this world needs,
no need to cook up fictitious stories!
There is no Christ but you.

71.
Cosmos courses in your corpuscles,
You don't need no writ, holy or otherwise.
You are holiness absolute,
ultimate answer to the brutes -
Christ is never afraid to be crucified!

72.
You are the Christ, you are the cross.
If you don't see, it's a cosmic loss.
Nature sends you a human,
Nature takes you a human,
Yet you bicker over identity fictitious.

73.

Nature sends you as human,
Nature takes you as human.
Yet you spend the entire journey,
least aware of the human duty,
chasing fear, myth and delusion!

74.

There is fear that makes us alert,
There is fear that ruins our heart.
Fear tamed does a lot of good,
Own your fear as sapiens should.
Untamed fear pours the veins with dirt.

Part 13

75.
Veins are meant to carry valor,
Don't let them vilified by fear.
Fear is a healthy part of psyche,
to make us cautious of tragedy,
but fear is never a civilized driver.

76.
Most fear is rooted in imagination,
an involuntary survival mechanism.
Fear will come, you can't help it,
It's okay to be scared stiff,
But then remember, you are a human.

77.
Fear may be a part of fervor,
It is not the whole of fervor.
Acknowledge all suggestions,
don't submit to assumptions.
All assumptions are dehumanizer.

78.
Unchecked baggage of bigotry
drags the clock back millions of years.
Unchecked biases, fear and prejudice,
despite all acts of science and policy,
revert consciousness into compost.

79.
Real change comes from individual realization,
It can't be imposed by forces authoritarian.
Build castles in the air all you want,
to enforce order and conduct -
you still cannot legislate civilization.

80.
Correction is the difference
between consciousness and compost.
Tradition that demonizes correction,
isn't worth civilized consideration.
Flawlessness is a construct of fiction.

Part 14

81.

Not time but rigid conservatism turns
consciousness into compost.
Fundamentalism and nationalism
turn the brain into broccoli.
Rigidity is the issue, not texts divine.

82.

Neither faith nor reason is the problem,
Real problem is lack of balance.
Extreme of faith and extreme of reason,
are both equally dangerous and inhuman.
Life unplastic is life unsapient.

83.
I can think sound, feel sane, and behave human,
because I have no allegiance.
Sectarianism turns mind into manure,
unfit to develop a human core.
World's greatest curse is sectarian allegiance.

84.
I feel so lonely,
amidst all dead loyalty.
This ism and that ism,
all isms are abandonism.
Abandon not, our one humanity!

85.
Your culture is my culture is world culture.
Each other's keeper we, together we're world maker.
We cause darkness, we bear the light.
Dawn comes at our will, at our will night.
Each other's torch we, together we're lightbringer.

86.
Togetherness is the light,
Separateness is night.
Hand in hand at heart,
Enhanced by taintless trust,
We wake up to real civil sight.

Part 15

103

87.

You are the key to my freedom,
You are the key to my calm.
You believe in good and evil spirits,
I believe in good and evil human beliefs.
Why must it force either of us to harm!

88.

You love your one "flawless scripture",
I love but all scriptures, despite flaws.
I am mindful of all their follies,
but also of their potent profundity.
Flawed goodness is far better
than imaginary goodness without flaws.

Sonnet of Flaws (1254)

Seek for literature without flaws,
You'd have no literature.
Seek for culture without flaws,
You'd have no culture.

Seek for science without flaws,
You'd have no science.
Seek for sapiens without flaws,
You'd have no sapiens.

Seek for friends without flaws,
You shall remain friendless.
Seek for humanity without flaws,
You'll freeze to death in flawlessness.

Flaws are our greatest source of forte,
Flawlessness facilitates blandness.
Correct where flaws cause blindness,
Embrace the flaws where they add sweetness.

89.

Flawless life is fragile life,
Flawed life is resilient life.
Greatest resilience is self-correction,
the seed of true civilization.
Flaws aware are instrument of flight.

90.

Life is not a math test,
where the answer is always binary.
Indeed life is no puny test,
Life is but a cosmic experiment,
conducted by the aware of humanity.

91.
Myth and magic are no more needed,
Real miracle is born of living breath.
Dead habits depend on delusion,
rooted in comforting descension.
Bold and aware, go rise a living legend!

92.
Human is needed, to be life's tether.
Human you are, o great myth maker!
Treading thorns under feet,
bearing mockery and deceit,
gallant awake, o globe galvanizer!

93.
Don't confuse gallantry with misdemeanor,
Don't confuse valor with bad behavior.
Revolution is an act of responsibility,
it is no act of reckless frivolity.
Vigor without virtue is pointless vigor.

94.
You gotta be your own doting parent,
You gotta be your own cautious guardian.
No one can teach you right from wrong,
morality is an act of self-correction -
born not of books, but of warm reason.

Part 16

95.
Give me a hundred minds,
bold, brave and kind,
the paradigm shall change,
despite stoneage resistance,
in the course of life and light.

96.
Light of progress is light of responsibility,
Light of justice is light of accountability.
Make policies all you want,
read and write decrees all you want,
there's no civilized world without plain empathy.

97.

Empathy is the only ethnicity,
Accountability is the only sanity.
All else is but fiction,
cooked up by superstition.
Only true race is inclusivity.

98.

Integration is civilization,
Kindness is the supreme reason.
It is more important to be kind,
than it is to be right.
Logic doesn't necessarily bring illumination.

Part 17

99.
Kindness is not a superpower,
Kindness is just a human power.
Superpowers are myth,
terms like charitable and altruist.
Only reality is everyday human power.

100.
Be kind because you are human,
not because you're charitable
or on a church mission.
Till kindness and humanness
are one and the same sentience,
no matter the exterior, you are no human.

101.
Kindness is poetry,
Reason is philosophy.
Philosophy is needed to sustain life,
Poetry is for what we stay alive.
Philosophy is aid, poetry is source energy.

102.
Women are poetry,
Men are philosophy.
Entire school of thought,
finds a voice undistraught,
in one little poetry.

103.

World needs poetry,
World needs philosophy.
Most times they are intertwined,
never to go their separate lines.
They are the antithesis of exclusivity.

104.

Poetry is the mightiest vessel for philosophy,
Poetry is the mightiest vessel for science.
Though I started out with prose,
I went through the poetic morph.
Now all my science is poetry,
all my poetry is philosophy.

Part 18

105.
Poetry is the literary form most potent,
Poetry is tether between life and intellect.
Intellect needs a mediator, poetry needs none.
Science needs a mediator, love needs none.
Love is the foundation, intellect mere servant.

106.
The intelligent may live a little,
But the lover is immortal.
Renounce your superstition,
then tame your reckless reason.
Mind, body, spirit, all are love's vessel.

107.
Mind, body, spirit,
they might sound three,
but they are actually one,
to fathom it you gotta unlearn,
all your inclinations of duality.

108.
Duality breeds disparity,
Oneness ends disparity.
Abandon all divide,
come together as one kind,
there shall be much less inhumanity.

109.

US Government is world's largest manufacturer
of disparity, depression and war.
Imperialism never went away,
it got disguised in diplomatic hay.
Hence, Russia is enemy, but not Israeli terror.

110.

Imperialism thrives on double standards,
Hypocrisy is but barbarians' first nature.
Enemy imperialist invades Ukraine,
Enemy is the villain.
Same standards don't apply
when Zionist friend is the invader.

Part 19

111.
Today I salute you,
for today you are king,
Ruler of the entire earth,
all its dust and its dirt,
yet an earth without a being.

112.
My congratulations, your majesty,
on your glorious accomplishment!
Yet fate worse than defeat,
for a creature at its peak,
is to be king without subjects.

The King
(A Sonnet - 1255)

Today I salute you,
For today you are king,
Ruler of the entire earth,
One without a living being.

My congratulations, your majesty,
On your glorious accomplishment!
Fate worse than a defeated king
is a king without subjects.

I got buried in the wreck,
So did my friends and family.
But still I salute you my king,
On your unparalleled victory.

I salute you from my grave,
For today you are king,
Ruler of a million lands,
Yet still, ruler of nothing!

113.

Soundbites don't make a sound society,
Apartheids don't heal humanity.
Without substance of character,
a heart that is lover not hater,
a loud mouth is not proof of sanity.

114.

Sanity is a simple enough word,
To practice it is not so much.
Hence insanity is so fashionable,
creating cults since time immemorial.
Sanity is too grand to be divided by cult.

115.

The day you make a cult of me
is the day you kill me.
The sun doesn't have a cult,
yet it lights up the world.
Live me natural, live me free -
Live me as air to humanity.

116.

Till peace becomes the human way,
defying all traditional sway,
and integration becomes sanity,
contrary to the norm of exclusivity,
all fancy ways will lead us astray.

Part 20

117.

The road won't make you feel one,
First feel one, then pick a road.
Without the vision of a decent being,
desiring unity with the world as kin,
no fancy road can bring you growth.

118.

Faith can do enormous damage,
So can our modern intelligence.
Unless they are guided by heart,
Both are but equally ignoramus.
Heartlessness is the original decadence.

119.
Love needs no translation,
for love is the translation.
Let love be your guide,
Let love ruin your sight.
Loveless sight is blind delusion.

120.
Delusion disguised as sense is still delusion,
Division disguised as faith is still division.
Problem is neither faith nor cleverness,
Real problem is intolerance.
Treat intolerance, and there'll be ascension.

Plenty Room For All
(The Sonnet - 1256)

Turban, Hijab, Habit or Tuxedo,
Wear whatever feels like second skin.
No need to justify to judgmental apes,
Life's too short to be wasted on fiends.

Let them just fade away,
as vestigials of evolution.
Savagery requires treatment,
not serious consideration.

To be treated as a human being,
One must behave as human being.
Faith, intellect, both are poison,
If the heart remains ever so mean.

There's plenty room for all thoughts,
No matter the measures of books 'n brain.
Fiction, reason, all are welcome,
On my earth where but love reigns.

121.
Love needs no gospel,
for love is the gospel.
How can you organize love,
How can you theorize love,
When love is indivisible!

122.
How do you organize the sun,
How do you organize the soil!
To even dream is sacrilege
of nature's borderless radiance.
We lose light in creedish turmoil.

Part 21

123.

Dead minds are cluttered with creed,
More alive in mind, lesser the creed.
It has nothing to do with fiction,
Forget even fancy talks of reason,
First you renounce all authoritarian heed!

124.

Not everything illogical is superstition,
Not everything logical aids civilization.
Facts and fiction both have a place,
in civilizing the world for human race.
To know their place, first you gotta be human.

125.
What is a human, what is a life?
There is no gospel to lifelight.
Life and creed don't go together,
Creed is the ultimate life destroyer.
Creed is but the end of all sight.

126.
Creed is the dust that ruins the heart,
Creed breeds but clouds of terror.
Talking of peace without removing creed,
is like sailing a boat with a hole beneath.
Dispersal of creed is ultimate peacemaker.

127.

If you want there to be peace,
You must first renounce all creed.
By creed I don't mean all belief,
I mean belief fundamentally divisive,
Those must alight from social steed.

128.

Bearing the baggage of ancestral foolery
is no honorous and civilized responsibility.
So you've got to choose,
will you make chains of your roots,
or step across historic primitivity!

Part 22

129.

What is a human, what is not?
Who is to decide, who is not?
No one but you,
gotta figure out the truth,
breaking the charm of second-hand thought.

130.

Tradition manufactures second hand humans,
Too much tradition breeds but stagnation.
Nothing organic is ever infallible,
yet scrutiny of tradition is contemptible.
Thus you sentence yourself to extinction.

131.
It's not the answer, it's the question.
Questions make the world go round.
Civilized society encourages question,
Stoneage society demonizes question.
Absence of question implies a mind unsound.

132.
Inquisitiveness is the sign of life osmosis,
Submissiveness is the sign of necrosis.
Don't know to question, don't know ascension.
Don't know curiosity, don't know realization.
The first sign of sanity is to be inquisitive.

133.

Don't confuse inquisitiveness with cynicism,
Inquisitiveness is a naive drive for learning.
Cynicism is an act of arrogant bitterness,
Inquisitiveness is a humble act of awareness.
Rationality without gentleness is most degrading.

134.

Rational mind is of no consequence,
If it loses its human grace.
Computers are a great tool,
To call it partner, I ain't no fool.
Head without heart is the ultimate disgrace.

Part 23

135.
Grace comes through humility,
Grace comes through community.
Community thrives on emotion,
nourished by compassionate reason.
Life ain't worth living on sheer logicality.

136.
Nobility of logic comes from heart,
Nobility of facts comes from heart.
Heartless brain is as dangerous
as brainless heart, or more perhaps.
Hence, develop your brain,
but on the grounds of heart.

137.
To err is machine,
To correct is mind.
To obey is animal,
hence we are so gullible,
While to question is sight.

138.
There is not one but two sight,
Animal sight and human sight.
Animal sight is instinctual,
and drives convenient survival,
Human sight often worsens strife.

139.
Hardship of justice is far more honorable
than kinship of disparity comfortable.
Bending your animal spine
to acquire disparity's kind,
is the antithesis of a life honorable.

140.
If your sense of justice and freedom
starts and ends with instagram,
you are not an activist,
you are just a circus act -
you are just an empty inhuman.

Part 24

141.

Justice restricted to social media,
is but make believe justice.
Accountability that leans
outside the comfort of screen,
is but new age prejudice.

142.

Social media is merely an extension
of real life, not a substitution.
Life that starts and ends
with social media trends,
is but ATP desecration.

143.
ATP is not only Adenosine triphosphate
but also Accountable Transformative Potential.
When such organic wonder is used,
to facilitate a tradition of feud,
it is the ultimate sacrilege, most despicable.

144.
Scriptures are no measure of sanctity,
Scriptures are no measure of sacrilege.
Sanctity and sacrilege manifest
in everyday human actions.
If you can't tell life from scripture,
you are already dead.

145.
Message always takes preference over rhyme,
Hence often my limericks do not rhyme.
Yet if all you care about is rhyme,
Naskar is not your cup of lime,
You are better off with your poems of slime.

146.
There's a whole real world outside your bubble,
Which you shall never live while you're in denial.
Renounce such archaic make believe,
that keeps you from life's wholeness.
Renouncing all comforting fallacy,
we shall rise indestructible.

Part 25

147.
Nothing physical is indestructible,
What is born must die, no matter the mettle.
So, focus not too much on physicality,
Focus instead on mental existentiality,
for the light of mind lingers
through space time continuum.

148.
Life is but electrochemistry.
No chemistry, no electricity.
So long as there is awareness
somewhere out there in deep space,
you just might touch them
with your electric memory.

149.
Life is but electrochemistry,
Humanity, responsible electrochemistry.
Wherever there is chemical reaction,
there is possibility of life ascension.
Ascension comes through living, not mimicry.

150.
It is one thing to value memory,
another to be a living mimicry.
I say living, but actually,
it's just lifeless vanity,
chasing comfort in dead history.

151.

Lift your sail, wind is afoot,
Step out of your dead habit hood.
Love is giving call,
Can't you hear at all!
When will you walk the living truth!

152.

All time bears fragments of truth,
But no time is the whole of truth.
Till you get this simple fact,
breaking the spell of stoneage tact,
you are just a host to hate and feud.

Part 26

153.
Truth is love, love is truth,
All else is but second truth.
Love is second to none,
for love is all and one.
Good facts must but aid lovetruth.

154.
I am love, you are love,
distance inbetween is just
illusion of the past,
keeping us apart,
never to realize, all is but love.

155.
There is no space, there is no time.
Lifeline is essentially loveline.
Borders are myth,
Orders are myth.
The ultimate order is our heartline.

156.
There is a chord from my heart to yours,
You cannot see in the mist of choirs.
Put an end to deadly choirs,
set sail for the living shores,
thus you learn to wield the oars.

157.
There is no handbook to civilization,
Handbooks only set forth uncivilization.
My handbook against yours,
your handbook against another's,
thus all handbooks cause but devastation.

158.
Learn from anything and everything,
Yet pledge allegiance to no one and nothing.
Allegiance is antithesis of civilization,
no matter the logic and motivation.
Logic behind division is the ultimate unreason.

Part 27

159.
Love is reason, hate is unreason.
Unity is reason, divide is unreason.
Think of all the logic you want,
to support your cause of mistrust,
in the absence of love all logic is treason.

160.
Hate is logic of the animal,
Heart is logic of the human.
This simple truth shall reveal,
your intent and your zeal.
Save love there is no motivation.

161.
God is your motivation! Okay.
Science is your motivation! Okay.
What do you do with that,
how do you lift the world!
What's your gift to the life most lay!

162.
Spreading scripture is not faithwork,
Mumbling facts is not sciencework.
True faith is kindness,
True science is service.
It takes a human to do lifework!

163.

Lifework is lightwork,
Cast aside all superstitious muck!
Old age superstition,
new age superstition,
neither can raise us up.

164.

Worse than the dark is pretend light,
Make believe light only extends the night.
If you want sight, embrace discomfort,
defying all spells of charming fraud,
then you just might have a taste of sight.

Part 28

165.

Beware Humankind! Unless you are careful,
your greatest achievement
will be your ultimate downfall.
In the mindless pursuit of nourishing
the money bank and tech bank,
human society shall run out of racebank.

166.

If you carry on like this, the day shall come,
you shall forget what it is to be human.
All this imperialist moronity,
sometimes commercial, sometimes military,
ultimately achieves nothing but destruction.

167.
In the pursuit of piling up gold,
all shall end up six feet under.
Till you change this heinous habit,
all this stupidity most selfish,
all the gold and all the silicon
won't avert the imminent disaster.

168.
Just when you lose regard for nature,
taking pride in your limitless power,
one small blow,
will wreck your fancy road!
Sanitarium awaits for the
self-proclaimed masters of nature.

169.
Not fear, but respect,
that is nature's requirement.
Fragile species like humans,
shouldn't boast over-confidence -
mightier species than us have failed the test.

170.
It's the smart who act most stupid,
for their smartness clouds their kilt*.
Those who think they rule the world,
with their money or their smarts,
are the new sickness, by the name of elite.

(*kilt is simply used as a poetic
alternative to pants)

Part 29

171.

Elitism is new fundamentalism,
which causes just as much division.
Moreover it freezes the world,
with its fancy intellectual lark.
Thus brain becomes the instrument
of new-age authoritarianism.

172.

Brain used to peddle division,
is brain wasted in vain.
Brain must be used
to end all myth-born feud.
Brain divisive is brain insane.

173.
Myths are a distortion of truth,
a corrupt exaggeration of truth.
One grain of truth in a bucket of lies,
facilitates but disease-carrying flies.
Truth begins with recognition of untruth.

174.
No truth is absolute,
No truth is supreme truth.
Truth is an eternal onion,
layer after layer of contemplation,
each but prelude to the next layer of truth.

175.
If you want to be an explorer of truth,
Learn to be comfortable with discomfort.
Vegetables submit to convenience,
we are the explorers of inconvenience.
Hardship wakes us up to vision uncharmed.

176.
We live under the spell of lies,
Dreaming of truth in a bed of lies.
With lies as our bedrock,
Sleep has become our curse.
Time to wake up 'n greet mind with mind!

Mirror Mind
(The Sonnet - 1257)

Sentience of a distant space,
I stand at your starry doorstep.
Born of carbon this simple life,
I come bearing a thread of love lace.

When will I meet my mirror mind,
When will I meet a mirror of kind!
Will all this struggle count for nothing,
Coming all this way, how can I alight!

I dreamt of you in my fiercest nights,
I craved for you in my suffering frights.
I ached for you on my brightest flights,
I trekked the galaxy seeking your sight.

Yet I remain ever so thirsty,
to drench in your monsoon smile.
When will I come to part with
this horrific state of divide!

Part 30

177.
Sentience of a distant space,
I stand at your starry doorstep.
Born of carbon
this simple lifeform,
I come bearing a thread of love lace.

178.
When will I meet my mirror mind,
When will I meet a mirror of kind!
Will all this struggle
count for nothing at all,
Coming all this way, how can I alight!

179.
I dreamt of you in my fiercest nights,
I craved for you in my suffering frights.
I ached for you with bouts of cries
on my brightest flights,
I trekked the galaxy seeking your sight.

180.
Yet I remain ever so thirsty,
to drench in your monsoon smile.
When will I come to part with,
this torment and grief,
this horrific state of divide!

181.
My love isn't hip, my love isn't pop.
My love isn't sold at pharmacy countertop.
I am too gone in love to look for pride,
Disreputation can't pierce my stubborn hide.
Bonkers I yell my heart out from the rooftop.

182.
Awake, aloud, engulf the world -
with a bonkers heart brimming with love.
Take the universe into arms -
No point of chest, without trust!
Every breath is declaration of my drunken love.

Part 31

183.
Breaths are declaration of love,
Not a second exists without love.
Till time and love are one,
Till life and love are one,
What's the point of all stories of love!

184.
How long will you chase love stories!
Unfold your own tales of tenacity.
How long will you glorify the fictitious rose,
overlooking those underneath your nose!
When will you nurture your own little nursery!

185.
Travel fast as light or not, doesn't matter.
Travel slow but with love, that's enough!
Motion of body doesn't matter,
Mind is the mightiest mover.
Live slow, but at full capacity of love.

186.
Inclusion is a fancy word for love,
Justice is a fancy word for love.
Where there is no love,
we cook up much fancy words.
Let there be love, and words will halve.

187.

There is no hashtag to rains,
Yet the monsoon comes regardless.
More the hashtags, less the justice.
More the stories, less the experience.
Swim o brave sailor, in love wordless!

188.

Love is not the word,
Life is not the word.
Truth is not the word,
Light is not the word,
Heart is not the word.

Part 32

189.
So many words, so little decency!
So many humans, so little humanity!
How could this be,
in a civilized society!
How could imitations undermine sanity!

190.
The world is awash with imitations,
Descriptions have garnered all attention.
Meantime, the depicted is unknown,
lived by a few walking alone,
while imitations bathe in celebration.

191.
Imitations won't do my dear,
Life of forgery will do no more!
Utter your own thoughts,
flutter your wings upward.
Second hand flight will
drag us all to eternal woe.

192.
Worry is a part of life,
Own your worries worth the life.
If you must fear,
choose your own original fear!
Entertain no infection
of society's shallow strife!

193.
Struggle of one is the struggle of all,
But learn to distinguish genuine struggle.
Phony struggles of the privileged
are not your concern my friend.
Use your life wisely to wipe real tears of trouble.

194.
Struggles of the privileged are easily visible,
for the society moves round self-serving dongles.
There is a whole world outside privilege,
full with real struggle beyond the trends.
Won't you step up to serve that world,
as the very first human incorruptible!

Part 33

195.
Life selfish is already corrupt,
Death unselfish is the immortality pact!
Be ready to die brave for a reason,
instead of living as vermin treason.
Life's first breath is breath given up.

196.
Breath sacrificed is first breath of life,
There is no such thing as a breath selfish.
If you are unselfish, then you're breathing.
If you are unselfish, then you're living.
Self separate from world, is life gone amiss.

197.
End of self is the birth of self,
When the world is contained in self.
There is no self and other,
there is no love and other.
Love, life, world, it's all one self.

198.
One is all, all is one.
Faces are plenty, life is one.
We look different,
we speak different.
Yet in pain and joy we feel all one.

199.

Universal language of pain is tear,
Universal language of joy is smile.
All other languages are secondary,
never to be given greater priority,
over the universal worth of human life.

200.

If smiles were currency,
if tears were treasury,
we'd live far better,
simple outside and simple interior,
without the divisive customs of fallacy.

Part 34

201.
Yet I acknowledge your need for fancy ways,
Only if you acknowledged the need for human ways,
In simplicity world would've found felicity,
denouncing all self-centric disparity,
world would've ushered into actual civilized ways.

202.
So far civilization is but a myth,
peddled by commercial elites,
a myth rooted in selfishness,
making a lot of policy noise,
which monetizes the lack of bliss.

203.
Simple world is a blissful world,
Fancy world is a depressed world.
Hence you need an army of therapists,
as crutches to your existential paralysis,
and the entire world is stuck in a warring pit.

204.
The ultimate world war is self war,
where the human fights the animal interior.
If you can rise triumphant in this war,
taming your spine crunching fear,
that's the beginning of the end of all outer war.

205.
End of self is the end of war,
For self conquered is world conquered.
With the self containing the world,
all sides simply converge,
for all sides of border are equally ours.

206.
I am neither pacifist nor socialist,
I am just not an animal elitist,
to conform to the status quo,
aloof from all living woe,
I am no make believe idealist.

Part 35

207.
Love is not idealism,
Peace is not idealism.
It's all but life,
I'm talking about human life.
What does an ape know to live beyond ism!

208.
I am human, hence I choose love.
I am human, hence I discard conquest.
You monkeys may try to continue,
with your primitivity most shrewd,
still you shall find this one human
as your ultimate impediment.

209.
Dear apes of earth planet,
I permit your stupidity harmless,
but so much as dream of harm,
lovingly I'll put you in your pram.
Humans are but guardians of the apes.

210.
Apes may have the luxury for inhumanity,
Human must stand parent to all primitivity.
If an ape commits inhumanity, it's animal nature.
If a human tolerates inhumanity, it's far worse.
Never O Human, abandon your duties to
humanity!

211.

Human you are, human you must stand.
Sleep not, slacken not, forgetting heartstance.
Heart is the way, heart is wayfarer.
Heart is love, heart is the lover.
Gather the civilized guts to reject
stoneage inheritance.

212.

Inheritance is not identity,
Savages run after such identity.
Civilized beings build out loud
their identity from the ground.
Real humans need no ancestry.

Part 36

213.
Ancestry is for the animals,
Ancestry is for the brainless.
You got a brain and heart,
put them to use at large.
Bloodline bears glory only
for the mindless and spineless.

214.
You got a mind, you got a spine.
Put them to use, as world's lifeline.
Our world is in our care,
bearing all sniggering and snare.
Never let your heart bend to animalkind.

215.
Tribes are for animals,
Divides are for animals.
If you are a human,
life lies in assimilation,
Never you worship animal shackles!

216.
Shackles are for savages,
Which they worship as roots.
When roots become chains,
life's wasted in vain.
Life's too short to waste as fools!

217.
Fools stay wrapped up in roots,
then yell, why is there so much feud!
For once, look in the mirror,
acknowledge the impact of your error,
then you might find the peace prelude.

218.
Roots are the prelude to chains,
Chains are the prelude to hate.
Break the spell of roots,
let your mind rise nude.
Thus you weave your own sentience.

Part 37

219.
Civilization come from the individual,
Individual is mother of civilization.
Individual means being free
from all ancestral spree.
Ancestors may be a part of our past,
they are not the route to our aspirations.

220.
Our ascension is our decision,
No dead roots can take such living decision.
Life's laws must be dictated by the living,
instead of nostalgically bowing and scraping.
Truth of life must unfold in living aspiration.

221.
Aspire for life as the living,
Never you mind the dead foreboding!
Fears of the past
must be left to the past.
Don't carry them around like vermin.

222.
When you carry fears from the past,
Past becomes a playground of disease.
Humans are to carry love and joy,
Why do you bow to the hateful ploy!
You are born to infect the world with peace.

223.

There is good infection, there is bad infection.
There is good intoxication, there's bad intoxication.
Drunken in the fumes of love,
walk around infecting all with love.
Route to peace goes through self-determination.

224.

There is no policy for peace but one,
It's that you gotta be nonsectarian.
Humans oughta live as human,
Is it too much of an imposition!
If so, jungle is the place for the inhuman.

Part 38

225.
Toys of war have changed,
Motivation remains ever so same.
Whether you carry spears or nuke,
you are still a stoneage brute,
till you break your trance of armament.

226.
Smashing rocks together to set a tribe on fire,
or breaking the atom to set a nation on fire,
It is all just the same,
prehistoric practices of savages insane.
How can humans declare such stupidity
as freedom-loving desire!

227.
Freedom has been the excuse for war,
Freedom is the byword of every conqueror.
Calling savagery as act of freedom,
doesn't bring about civilization,
it only sustains the paradigm of disaster.

228.
It's a terrible state of affairs,
when apes cause more disaster than nature.
When more people die
as victims of some prehistoric lie,
it's time to rewrite our life's parameter.

229.
Life that causes nothing but death,
is no living but the dead.
To live is to love,
to love is to serve,
where does invasion come into all this!

230.
If you must invade, invade hearts.
If you must steal, steal sorrows.
Let your love spread across the world,
Respond cries of the souls unheard.
If you must conquer, conquer the world's woes.

Part 39

231.

Life begins at the end of tribe,
Time begins at the end of fright.
To wake up from animal sleep,
you gotta put prejudice to sleep.
Peace begins at the end of tribe.

232.

Peace begins at the end of prejudice,
Mind begins at the end of malice.
Time begins at the end of fear,
till then all time breeds but war.
World begins when all lands are one piece.

233.
Pieces ruin peace.
One piece, one peace.
When pieces are priority,
over and above humanity,
a thousand UN won't bring peace.

234.
Person is the source of peace,
Person is the source of harmony.
When the person is savage,
even in this day and age,
no use of conjuring a ton of policy.

235.
Peace is a matter of civilian responsibility,
It is not a matter of brainy argumentation.
Then how do we bring about change,
in a world so fundamentally savage -
only through internal education.

236.
We need a new kind of education,
that instills accountability
not mere information.
It is no use,
memorizing bookish truths,
if the heart is blind to the
suffering of the fellow human.

Part 40

237.
Throw away such books that make you selfish,
Throw away such education teaching tricks of malice.
Education founded on competition,
is but mental malnutrition.
such education only changes the shape of prejudice.

238.
Education must equip the mind with tools,
to transform this age-old paradigm of fools.
What's the point of learning facts,
if you can't wipe your neighbor's tears,
you might as well walk with a skull full of stool.

239.
On our neck we carry a brain,
unparalleled among all the animals.
Yet we haven't learnt
to use it for a better reason,
than same old competition of tribals.

240.
Tribe, tribe, tribe and tribe,
All we have is loyalty of tribe!
Tribes of different size and shape,
none shows the sign of unified sentience,
yet we call ourselves sapiens with sight!

241.
This you call sight,
then what is nonsight!
This you call civility,
then what is uncivility!
If this is light, what is night!

242.
There is plenty to learn about light,
and there is no light till you rise above tribe.
We are humans, our tribe, humanity.
We are vessels of light, our religion, empathy.
There is no civilization till you unlearn
your ways uncivilized.

Part 41

243.
Ways of the dead,
look good in the grave.
What are you doing
with ways of the rotten!
Why are you mimicking the dead!

244.
Mimicry of the dead,
buries the world in grave.
We've been digging long enough,
isn't it time to end this muck -
isn't it time to bury all ways divided!

245.
Our world our ways,
Our ways as in living ways.
Gone to grave,
leave in grave,
don't push the living in graves.

246.
Graves are not our home,
Graves are not our destiny.
Home of the living
is heart of the living.
Let no gravelover dictate living sanity.

247.

I permit you peace in grave,
but don't come offering
suggestions from the grave.
Sanity is a matter of life,
burn your damn textual strife!
Let dead ancestors lie,
without glorifying their mistakes.

248.

The living need no ancestral consent
on how to think, feel and behave.
Each generation must carve their life
based on new reason of their time,
while in heart their feet are firmly rooted.

249.
Root yourself in heart not grave,
Root your breath in benevolence.
Whenever they charge at you,
with their decrees most crude,
treat them with care as their parent.

250.
I am an equal brother to the human,
But the godparent to the inhuman.
I won't harm the savages,
But will obstruct their advances.
I am a friend to those with mind,
but guardian to the moron.

Part 42

251.
Guardian of life is the living.
Living world, rules of the living!
I am alive,
you are alive,
we decide the parameters of living.

252.
Gentle giants are needed,
Hearty Himalayas are needed -
with electrolyte sweat
that electrifies the world beyond hate,
Conscientious Kilimanjaros are needed!

253.
Kevlar for hide,
Titanium for spine.
Take the leap,
beyond the creed -
Awake, arise, o humankind!

254.
There is no advancement,
till the heart advances.
Even if we land a rocket,
on other planets,
it means nothing till we
nourish earth with humanness.

Part 43

255.
Can't take care of life on earth,
What's the point of traveling to stars!
No matter where the savages go,
they shall cause death and sorrow.
Find the light within, before
you dream of the stars.

256.
It's easy to conquer stars,
not so much to humanize earth.
It's easier to invent warp drive,
than it is to generate heart-drive.
Space is just plan b for earth's traitors.

257.
Oligarchs are turning space exploration
into yet another frontier of imperialism.
Horrors faced by humans on earth,
will soon be exported to the stars,
unless the civilians crush all
oligarchic aspiration.

258.
Where do oligarchs come from?
They come from people's shallowness.
When people stop being shallow,
no oligarch shall get to grow,
to spread their life-crushing tentacles.

259.
If the humans behaved responsibly,
there would be no oligarchy.
But when you can't tell necessity,
from life's basic amenity,
you empower oligarchs beyond all sanity.

260.
Next time you glorify some entrepreneur,
Take stock of some of your brain power.
You might just be able
to prevent society being crippled,
by the exploits of the privileged from the sewer.

Part 44

261.
Privilege is the sewer,
that turns the world into sewer,
where the privileged live well,
while rest of humanity struggle,
to afford the essentials of survival.

262.
It's okay to live a little better,
to entertain little fancy desires.
But when the world struggle in slums,
while you lie in your mansion,
it's a crime of astronomical proportions.

263.
Life and luxury must never go together,
When they do, disparities appear.
Economy erected on disparity
rewards endeavors of greedy atrocity.
With such paradigm you want growth to appear!

264.
Class-based growth is fall of civilization,
Disparity-powered progress is prelude to extinction.
Grab hold of your abundance,
redirect your excess resources,
towards initiatives of collective ascension.

265.
Oligarchs and wannabe oligarchs teach you
to invest in stocks and bonds, without clue.
That's how they feed on your insecurity,
and in the process fuel the disparity,
that makes them richer at the expense of fools.

266.
I say, forget all nonsense of wealth!
Securing basics, give the rest in help.
Without expecting profits,
invest in small businesses,
that's how you build a sustainable planet.

Part 45

267.
There are plenty ways
to use your excess resources.
Forget wealth and think of help,
how you can live humanly best.
Thus you cripple imperial advances.

268.
Lesser the needs, more the sustainability.
More the needs, more the imperialist atrocity.
Be simple and live simple,
thus you rise incorruptible.
Only through such individuals
world will know humanity.

269.
Simplicity brings sustainability,
Luxury facilitates atrocity.
When you are simple,
the whole world is well.
Simplicity is the road to recovery.

270.
Simplicity is the road to recovery,
recovery from all man-made disparity.
Economy that rewards selfishness,
is but a glorified criminal offense.
Hypocrisy never brings sustainability.

271.
No matter how much you yell and worry,
from your comfortable tower of ivory,
till you become one with all,
sharing the last bread amongst all,
there is no question of civilized society.

272.
Wearing suits don't make you civilized,
Speaking fancy don't make you civilized.
How far will you go for the fallen,
will you rise to lift human condition,
that is the actual trillion dollar question!

Part 46

273.

Till the commoner becomes reformer,
and riots against rigidity,
there is no peace,
there is no progress,
there is no sustainability.

274.

Till the commoner becomes reformer,
and roars against disparity,
there is no reason,
there is no inclusion,
there is no civilized society.

275.
Till the world citizen becomes world leader,
and stands unbent up to imperialist empires,
there is no health,
there is no harmony,
there is no equal accessibility.

276.
Equal access is possible,
when all are self-enabled,
but when enablers are the privileged,
aloof from everyday problems,
policies are but half-cocked disastricles.

277.
Sustainable development goals are but a facade,
If there is no civilian accountability underneath.
What will you do with your policy,
What will you do with your legality,
When you can't do nothing when things get desperate!

278.
Russia invaded Ukraine, what did your policy do?
Israel invaded Palestine, what did your policy do?
Billionaires screw commoners on a daily basis,
while keeping your policymakers in pocket,
what exactly do your policy do?

279.
When civilians are savage as neanderthals,
policies achieve nothing lasting.
Remove the law for a single day,
you'll find the animal in civilian face.
That's what you call change through policy?

280.
If this is what your policy achieves,
you are better off with a dictatorship.
If the civilians can't tell right from wrong,
without authoritarian intervention,
it's not society but house of lunatics.

281.
That's why my work is with the civilians,
I got nothing to do with law and policy.
Civilians awake,
civilians arise,
time awaits to witness your accountability.

282.
Be accountable, be sensible,
out of your own sense and will.
All other sense is nonsense,
common sense is supreme sense,
with it shall civilization heal.

283.
To heal or not to heal,
that's the real question of zeal.
How much you care,
how much you dare,
determine if the world shall heal.

284.
Only people can heal the world,
not a bunch of policy most drab.
Sure policy has a place,
but only the second place,
second to actual civic sense.

Part 48

285.

When civic sense and common sense combine,
No force can keep the world from light.
Where there is civilian accountability,
there is no need for policy,
hence there is no question of corruption.

286.

When you give all power to law and policy,
it opens a gateway to bureaucratic corruption.
But when the civilians are transformed,
corruption turns powerless and can do no harm.
Only policy needed is that of self-determination.

287.
Focus on transforming civilians,
rather than spoon feeding responsibility.
You can't keep the society in nappies,
till the world gets buried in disparity.
It's time to abandon the crutches
that keep you cripple.

288.
Training wheels are for the children,
Yet we kept a society moving on training wheels.
No wonder prejudice is so rampant,
more than reason rigidity is dominant.
How can you walk if you're addicted to crutches!

289.
When the whole world is addicted
to different kinds of mental crutches,
you can dream of peace and love
all you want in your castle of glass,
that does nothing for sapiens progress.

290.
Progress requires self-determination,
abandoning reliance on external forces.
Counterfeit progress
only postpones the troubles,
thus even in this day and age
the world burns in intolerance.

Part 49

291.
Where do you think intolerance comes from?
Intolerance is born of ideological allegiance.
Allegiance of any kind,
practically peddles but divide,
conditioning the mind against its own wholeness.

292.
Mind without wholeness
leads to a world of intolerance.
Be whole in mind,
bowing to no creed unkind,
lo, you become antidote to intolerance.

293.
Vaccines prevent viral outbreak,
Wholeness prevents outbreak of hate.
When you are whole,
the world beats in your soul,
bigotry runs out of vessels to infect.

294.
Virus cannot spread without carrier,
Bigotry cannot spread without carrier.
Love is the ultimate vaccine,
against all hate, both seen and unseen.
Once you're vaccinated hate will soon disappear.

295.
Vaccinated with love,
boosted with reason,
mind becomes a powerhouse,
enough to power the world house,
putting an end to all discrimination.

296.
Corruption, hate, prejudice, bigotry,
all fester due to civilian unaccountability.
When you stand boldly on duty
as an accountable citizen of society,
you are the ultimate answer
to all humanitarian calamity.

Part 50

297.
Society is the question,
Society is the answer.
And since you are society,
you are that mythical key,
to all troubles of society.

298.
Commoners are the makers of society,
Commoners are the keepers of society.
Depend on neither law nor politics,
to fix your every little troubles,
it's your world, to fix it
is your responsibility.

299.
Once civilians take charge of society,
unarmed, with just spinal electricity,
tyrants will tremble at your sight,
oligarchs will crumble to your might,
the universe will conspire
at your will and sanity.

300.
Sanity is a simple enough word,
But the responsibility hangs heavy.
Do justice to the title sapiens,
Build a world you never got by inheritance.
Calamity to chaos, you are the order to humanity.

Epilogue

I have but one law - I don't exist. I don't have a homeland, I don't have a native tongue, I don't have an origin culture - for you are my home, your tongue is my tongue, your culture is my culture. Those who still want to learn about my origin, could easily find out where I come from and all that nonsense, but as for me, my existence is rooted in you - that's all you gotta know. Nothing else matters, nothing else must matter. I repeat, nothing else must matter. For an earthbound species, I am native of earth - for an interplanetary species, I am native of Milky Way - for an intergalactic species, I am a native of the cosmos - for a lifeform beyond time and space, I am but a speck of carbon-based electrochemical memory.

www.ingramcontent.com/pod-product-compliance
Lightning Source LLC
Chambersburg PA
CBHW051038250726
48656CB00001B/33